UNSOLVED MYSTERIES

GHOSTS

BY ORLIN RICHARD

Halfmoon
Moe Road
New York

ABOUT THE AUTHOR

Orlin Richard is a writer and editor from Fargo, North Dakota. He wants to come back and haunt the library as a ghost so he never has to stop reading books.

Published by The Child's World©
1980 Lookout Drive • Mankato, MN 56003-1705
800-599-READ • www.childsworld.com

ACKNOWLEDGMENTS
The Child's World©: Mary Berendes, Publishing Director
Red Line Editorial: Editorial direction
The Design Lab: Design
Amnet: Production

DESIGN ELEMENT: Shutterstock Images

PHOTOGRAPHS ©: Annette Shaff/Shutterstock Images, cover; Cylla Von Tiedemann/DK Images, 6; Everett Historical/Shutterstock Images, 8; Rachel Blaser/Shutterstock Images, 11; Rob Cole Photographic/iStockphoto, 12; Sir Simon Marsden/The Marsden Archive/Alamy, 14; iStockphoto, 17, 21, 23; Bettmann/Corbis, 19

ISBN 9781634070737
LCCN 2014959758

Printed in the United States of America
Mankato, MN
July, 2015
PA02266

TABLE OF CONTENTS

2792

GHOSTLY ENCOUNTERS

In August 1956, Charles Edmunds and his family moved to a new home. It was the Mackenzie House in Toronto, Canada. The house was old and beautiful. But soon, the family noticed strange noises and sights.

Edmunds heard loud footsteps, even when no one else was in the house. His son, Robert, also noticed unexplained sounds. Robert sometimes heard piano music at night. The family kept several potted plants. A water pitcher was next to the plants. Once, they came home to find mud smeared on the curtains. The mud was from the plant pots. Water from the pitcher had spilled onto the floor.

Mackenzie House was a historic home. William Lyon Mackenzie, the first mayor of Toronto, had lived there. The Edmunds family wanted to help preserve the house. But as time passed, the family grew scared. They saw eerie figures in the house. One was a woman in old clothes. Another was a man with a beard. According to the family, these people stood by their beds at night. During the day, they disappeared.

After four years, the Edmunds family moved away. They believed the Mackenzie House was haunted. They thought the strange figures were ghosts. Robert said the family was too scared to stay. Other caretakers took their place. Some also reported seeing ghosts.

Today, the Mackenzie House is a public museum. Visitors still notice strange sights in the house. Some see rocking chairs move by themselves. Others have reported seeing a ghostly man. He may be the same man the

Some visitors at the Mackenzie House report seeing ghosts.

Edmunds family saw. They think he is the ghost of William Lyon Mackenzie.

Are there really ghosts in the Mackenzie House? No one can say for sure. Many people visit the home hoping to find the truth.

What Is a Ghost?

A ghost is a dead person's **spirit**. Many people believe that a person's spirit is separate from the body. They think the spirit continues to live after the body dies.

Many people think that the spirits of the dead go to a new place. A ghost is a spirit that stays on Earth. Ghosts are also called phantoms or specters.

People have believed in ghosts for thousands of years. Homer was a Greek poet said to have lived in 800 BC. Ghosts appeared in his poem *The Iliad*. He described ghosts

During the 1800s, Washington Irving wrote ghost stories and other tales.

that look like shadows. In the poem, the ghosts disappear like **vapor**. Homer's ghosts talk to living people. They even tell the future.

Washington Irving wrote early American ghost stories. In "The Legend of Sleepy Hollow," he described a **spectral** man without a head. In the story, the headless man rides on a horse through the fields. He looks for his lost head. According to popular beliefs, many ghosts are looking for something. They need to find it before they can leave Earth.

Many people enjoy ghost stories. Yet no one has been able to prove that ghosts are real. Some say they have seen ghosts. But scientists often give other explanations for the sightings. Believers are not convinced. They think the spirits of the dead walk among us.

UNDERSTANDING GHOSTS

In almost every **culture**, some people believe in ghosts. Different cultures think about ghosts in different ways. In Mexico, people celebrate the Day of the Dead. Some believe that on this day, spirits of their dead ancestors come to visit Earth. Families offer gifts to make the spirits happy. A large number of people in the United Kingdom also believe in ghosts. But they link ghosts to very old houses and castles. Many British believers say they have never seen a ghost.

Cultures also share some ideas about ghosts. In many countries, people believe in kind ghosts and cruel ghosts. Kind ghosts protect loved ones. Cruel ghosts scare people.

Hauntings

According to stories, ghosts haunt places they know. Spirits stay in important places from their lives. Many ghosts reportedly haunt their former homes. Others haunt the places where they died.

Some believe that the Castle Keep in Newcastle, England, is haunted.

Often, ghosts are tied to people rather than places. Many people report seeing family members who passed away. Some are happy to see them. Seeing a loved one again can be comforting. Some people say these spirits protect them.

Why would ghosts want to visit living people? Believers have many theories. Perhaps the ghosts have unfinished business on Earth. Some may want revenge. Other ghosts could want to deliver messages. Some might need to finish tasks or jobs. And some may not want to leave Earth.

What Ghosts Look Like

Most say that ghosts do not have bodies. They may be invisible or **transparent**. Many people dress up like ghosts for Halloween. They wear white sheets. This may come from the practice of covering the dead in **shrouds**.

Some believe that ghosts show up in photographs. In 1936, photographers for *Country Life* magazine visited Raynham Hall in the United Kingdom. They took one picture of an old staircase. In the photograph, the filmy shape of a woman appears. Many claim that this shape is a ghost. Others say the photograph is a **hoax**. The photographers might have combined two pictures. This could create the appearance of a ghost.

Spots of glowing light sometimes show up on photographs. Believers say that these spots, or orbs, are

Many people thought this photograph showed a ghost in Raynham Hall.

ghosts. The orbs cannot be seen by the naked eye. Other explanations for the orbs are possible. The orbs could be light reflecting off dust in the air. Or the orbs might be errors from the process of developing the photographs.

Other Signs of Ghosts

Even if people do not see ghosts, they may report signs of them. There are many **phenomena** commonly connected to ghosts. People notice sudden drops in temperature. These are often known as "cold spots." Some notice unexplained smells. People hear thumps that sound like footsteps. Doors seem to open and shut on their own. Lights flicker. Music plays while the stereo is off. Voices are heard in an empty house.

These events are not proof of ghosts. Scientists give other explanations. But many people think ghosts are to blame.

INVESTIGATING GHOSTS

When people report ghost sightings, researchers investigate. Ghost hunters believe that ghosts are real. They try to find the ghosts and learn about them. **Skeptics** do not believe in ghosts. They investigate other possible causes for reported ghost sightings.

Hunting for Ghosts

Ghost hunters travel to places where ghosts have been reported. They research the locations. Have ghosts been sighted there in the past? What kinds of phenomena occurred? The ghost hunters use this information to prepare. Sometimes, families

hire ghost hunters. They ask the hunters to persuade ghosts
to leave their homes.

If ghosts have been seen, the hunters might bring film
equipment. They set up cameras all around the location.
They try to capture the ghosts on film. To hear ghost
sounds, the hunters set up recording equipment. Then

they look for possible sources of the sounds. If they cannot find a source, they believe a ghost could be present. Ghost hunters also interview witnesses. They gather information about the ghost sightings. Ghost hunters believe they can prove that ghosts exist. Some say they have talked to ghosts. Others say they have recorded how ghosts look or sound.

Yet there is still no clear evidence of ghosts. Ghost hunters' photographs tend to be blurry. Audio recordings are not clear. Because some past ghost sightings have been made up, new recordings might also be hoaxes.

Skeptics

Skeptics also study signs of ghosts. But they try to find scientific explanations for the signs.

One famous skeptic was Harry Houdini. He was a magician in the 1920s. Houdini set out to disprove

mediums. He learned how mediums pretended to talk to the dead. Then Houdini performed their acts. He showed how their tricks worked. Houdini convinced many people not to believe in mediums. Today, other skeptics disprove common ideas about ghosts.

Harry Houdini showed how some mediums pretended to talk to the dead.

Some false evidence is from mistakes, not tricks. People may be wrong about what they see and hear. Witnesses often say they see ghosts out of the corners of their eyes. Scientists have conducted research on **peripheral vision**. They know that people often make mistakes about what they see. They may think they see a person moving. In fact, what they see may be something completely different.

Many people report seeing ghosts in old buildings. Others see them in graveyards. They describe hearing strange footsteps in these places. Sometimes they hear ghostly voices. Believers say these places have a lot of history. As a result, they are more likely to have ghosts. But skeptics believe there are other explanations. Old houses sometimes have boards that creak. The creaking boards may sound like footsteps. Graveyards are full of shadows. The shadows might make people believe they have seen a ghost. Most people think of cemeteries as scary places. They might also consider old houses spooky. As a result, they may imagine that they see or hear ghosts.

Many ghost sightings occur in old houses.

Remaining Questions

Most scientists agree that ghosts are not real. But others disagree. Millions of people believe they have seen ghosts. Some say we do not have the tools to find ghosts yet. Scientists, skeptics, and ghost hunters continue to investigate sightings. Someday we may know the truth.

Glossary

culture (KUL-chur) The history and traditions of a group of people are its culture. In almost every culture, some people believe in ghosts.

hoax (HOHKS) A hoax is a false idea that people are tricked into believing. Some people create a photograph of a ghost as a hoax.

mediums (MEE-dee-umz) Mediums are people who claim to speak to the dead. Harry Houdini showed that some mediums were only pretending to speak to dead people.

peripheral vision (puh-RIF-ur-ul VIZH-un) Using peripheral vision means to see from the outer edge of a person's vision. Sometimes ghosts seem to appear in people's peripheral vision.

phenomena (fe-NOM-uh-nuh) Phenomena are events or facts that researchers can study. People have observed different phenomena related to ghosts.

shrouds (SHROWDZ) Shrouds are pieces of cloth used to cover a dead body. Wearing white sheets for ghost costumes looks like shrouds on dead bodies.

skeptics (SKEP-tiks) Skeptics are people who doubt certain ideas or explanations. Most skeptics do not believe that ghosts exist.

spectral (SPEK-trul) To be spectral is to be of or like a ghost. A spectral man haunts a town in "The Legend of Sleepy Hollow."

spirit (SPIHR-it) A spirit is a person's soul. Many believe that a person's spirit may live on after death.

transparent (tranz-PAIR-uhnt) When something is transparent, people can see through it. Ghosts are often described as being transparent.

vapor (VAY-pur) A vapor is a gas or fog. Some people believe that ghosts are made of vapor.

To Learn More

BOOKS

Guiley, Rosemary. *Ghosts and Haunted Places.* New York: Chelsea House, 2008.

Pipe, Jim. *The Twilight Realm: Ghosts.* New York: Gareth Stevens, 2014.

Zoehfeld, Kathleen Weidner. *Ghost Mysteries: Unraveling the World's Most Mysterious Hauntings.* New York: Aladdin, 2009.

WEB SITES

Visit our Web site for links about ghosts: **childsworld.com/links**

Note to Parents, Teachers, and Librarians: We routinely verify our Web links to make sure they are safe and active sites. So encourage your readers to check them out!

Index